# Rabbits and Coyotes

*Columbus, OH • Chicago, IL • Redmond, WA*

The **McGraw·Hill** Companies

# The First Reading Books

The *First Reading Books* are reading books that fill the need for easy-to-read stories for the primary grades. The interest appeal of these stories will encourage reading at the very beginning grade level.

The stories focus on the easier 110 words from the Dolch 220 Basic Sight Vocabulary and the 95 Common Nouns. Beyond these lists, the books use about two new words per page.

This series was prepared under the direction and supervision of Edward W. Dolch, Ph.D.

This revision was prepared under the direction and supervision of Eleanor Dolch LaRoy and the Dolch Family Trust.

## SRAonline.com

 SRA

Send all inquiries to:
SRA/McGraw-Hill
8787 Orion Place
Columbus, OH 43240-4027

Printed in the United States of America.

ISBN 0-07-602510-1

1 2 3 4 5 6 7 8 9 MAZ 12 11 10 09 08 07 06 05 04

# Table of Contents

# White Rabbit

Once there was a white rabbit. White Rabbit was very hungry. So she went to the garden to get some food.

White Rabbit took the food home, but when she got there, she could not get in.

Someone said, "Go away. I am Bad Goat. I am going to live in this house."

White Rabbit was very afraid. She went to Brown Cow.

"Brown Cow, will you help me?" asked White Rabbit. "Bad Goat will not get out of my house."

Brown Cow said, "I am afraid of Bad Goat. I cannot help you."

White Rabbit was very sad. She went to Big Dog.

"Big Dog, will you help me?" she asked. "Bad Goat will not get out of my house."

Big Dog said, "I am afraid of Bad Goat. I cannot help you."

White Rabbit cried. Then Little Ant came by. She said, "Why are you sad, White Rabbit?"

White Rabbit said, "Bad Goat will not get out of my house. No one will help me. I am sad."

Little Ant said, "I will help you. I will make Bad Goat get out of your house."

White Rabbit and Little Ant went back to the house.

White Rabbit said, "Bad Goat, get out of my house."

Bad Goat laughed. "I am Bad Goat," he said. "You cannot live here. I am going to live in this house."

Then Little Ant crawled under the door. Little Ant bit Bad Goat on the leg. Little Ant bit Bad Goat again.

Bad Goat cried, "Oh! Oh! Oh!"

Little Ant bit Bad Goat again, and Bad Goat ran out of the house.

White Rabbit said, "Little Ant, come and live with me."

And from that day on, Little Ant lived with White Rabbit.

# Rabbit and Monkey

Rabbit and Monkey were going down the road. They saw a man who had some bananas.

"I must have some of the man's bananas," said Monkey.

"How are you going to get the bananas?" asked Rabbit.

"You walk in the road so the man will see you," said Monkey. "I will go where he cannot see me."

Rabbit did what Monkey told him to do. The man saw Rabbit in the road. The man put down his bananas. Rabbit ran, and the man ran after him. Rabbit ran and ran, and the man did not catch him.

Monkey got the bananas. He took the bananas up in a tree. Soon he had eaten all of them.

When Rabbit got back to the road, there were no more bananas.

"Why are there no bananas for me?" asked Rabbit.

"I started to think the man would catch you," said Monkey.

Rabbit was very angry.

The next day Rabbit was in the grass by a hornets' nest. A hornets' nest is big and round. Little hornets live in it. They will fly out and sting you if they are angry.

Monkey came by and said, "Rabbit, why are you there in the grass? Come and play!"

"I cannot play," said Rabbit as he looked at the hornets' nest. "This is the king's drum. The king told me to look after it."

"Let me play the king's drum," said Monkey.

"Oh, no," said Rabbit. "The king would be very angry if I did."

"Let me play the king's drum," said Monkey.

"Monkey," said Rabbit, "it is your doing."

"It is my doing," said Monkey. And he played the hornets' nest like it was a drum. He played it with his two hands.

The angry hornets flew out of the nest. They tried to sting Monkey. Monkey ran away into the woods.

Rabbit laughed and laughed.

# Angry Little Rabbit

Once there was a little rabbit. He lived with his mother. Every morning Little Rabbit went out to look for food.

One day Little Rabbit came home very angry.

"Mother," he said, "I get up early. I go to the woods to look for food. But there is someone who gets there before I do."

Mother said, "Little Rabbit, you must get up very early."

The next morning Little Rabbit got up very early. He went to the woods to look for food. When he got back, he said to his mother, "I got up very early and went to the woods, but someone was there before me. I am going to get a net. I will catch the one who gets up before I do."

Mother said, "Little Rabbit, I am afraid you will catch something big. I am afraid it will not be good."

Little Rabbit got a big net. He went out to the woods and put up the net. Then he went home and went to sleep.

Early the next morning Little Rabbit went to the woods. He went to his net. In the net was the sun.

The sun was very angry. "You bad rabbit," the sun cried. "Get me out of this net, or I will burn up the woods."

Little Rabbit ran to the net. He let the sun out of the net, and the sun jumped into the sky. But the sun had burned Little Rabbit's fur. The fur on his back was white no more. It was burned brown.

Little Rabbit ran home to his mother. He told her how he had the sun in his net.

He told her how he had let the sun out of the net so it could go back to the sky.

"Oh, Little Rabbit," said his mother. She put something on his burned back to help Rabbit.

From that day to this, a rabbit you see in the woods will not have white fur on its back. It will have brown fur.

# Brown Rabbit and Jack Rabbit

Brown Rabbit was little. He lived in the mountains. In winter, when it snowed, his home was in a tree.

Jack Rabbit was big. He liked to run on the plains. He lived in a hole in the ground. In winter he liked to eat corn he got from a farmer.

One day in the winter, Jack Rabbit looked up at the mountains. "I wonder how my friend Brown Rabbit is doing," Jack Rabbit said to himself.

Brown Rabbit, up in the mountains, started to think of Jack Rabbit. "I wonder if my friend Jack Rabbit got food to eat," said Brown Rabbit to himself. "I do not want my friend to be hungry this winter."

So Brown Rabbit got some food. He started to go down the mountain to see his friend Jack Rabbit.

Down on the plains, Jack Rabbit said to himself, "I wonder if my friend Brown Rabbit is warm up in the snow."

Jack Rabbit got some wood. He was going to go up the mountain with it. He would make a fire so Brown Rabbit would be warm.

Brown Rabbit saw Jack Rabbit as he came up the mountain. Brown Rabbit had some food. Jack Rabbit had sticks of wood.

"Good morning," said Brown Rabbit. "I did not think I would see you on the mountain."

"Good morning," said Jack Rabbit. "I saw snow on your mountain. I wanted to see if you were warm."

"Oh, yes," said Brown Rabbit. "I am very warm in my house in the tree."

Then Brown Rabbit started to laugh. "My friend," he said, "I have food for you. I was afraid you were hungry."

"You are very good, my friend," said Jack Rabbit, "but I have food here on the plains. I can get corn from a farmer."

The rabbits laughed and laughed. Then Brown Rabbit and Jack Rabbit started to eat the food Brown Rabbit had.

# Coyote and Squirrel

After the sun was down, Coyote could not sleep, so he walked and walked. He looked for animals that could not sleep.

Rabbit's house was in the green grass. She, too, could not sleep. But when she saw Coyote walking by the grass, Rabbit jumped into her house.

Coyote had good eyes. He saw Rabbit jump into her house. "Rabbit is like all animals, and animals do not like me. They all run away," he said.

Duck's house was by the water. He, too, could not sleep. But when he saw Coyote walking by the water, Duck jumped into the water.

Coyote had good eyes. He saw Duck jump into the water. "Duck is like all animals, and animals do not like me. They all run away," he said.

Cow's house was at the farm. She, too, could not sleep. But when she saw Coyote walking by the farm, Cow jumped into the barn.

Yes, Coyote saw Cow jump into the barn too. "Yes," Coyote said, "Cow is like all animals, and animals do not like me. They will not talk to me. They all run away."

Coyote was sad. "I cannot sleep, and no animal will talk to me," he said.

Sad Coyote walked and walked. He saw a big tree. "I am too sad to walk. I will stop under the tree," he said.

Coyote had good eyes, but he did not see Squirrel. Squirrel was in the tree. Squirrel, too, could not sleep. Squirrel saw Coyote stop under the tree, but he did not jump away.

Under the tree, Coyote said, "Animals will not talk to me."

From up in the tree, Squirrel said, "I will talk to you!"

Coyote jumped. "Squirrel!" he said. "I did not see you up in the tree."

"Who will not talk to you, Coyote?" asked Squirrel.

"Rabbit, Duck, and Cow," said Coyote. "They do not like me."

"They are afraid of you," said Squirrel. "They are afraid you will eat them."

Coyote laughed and said, "Afraid! But I will not eat them!" He laughed and laughed.

"Good, but they will not talk to you," said Squirrel from up in the tree.

"You said you will talk to me, Squirrel," said Coyote.

"I will," said Squirrel. And Squirrel and Coyote did talk . . . and talk and talk.

After the long talk, Coyote said, "I will walk to my house and sleep. Thank you, Squirrel, for the talk!"

"Thank you," said Squirrel.

But before he walked away, Coyote asked, "Are you afraid of me, Squirrel?"

"You cannot get up in a tree, can you?" asked Squirrel.

"No, I cannot get up in a tree," said Coyote.

"As long as you cannot get up in a tree, I will not be afraid of you!" said Squirrel.

As Coyote walked away, he laughed and said, "Thank you, Squirrel."

# Coyote's Fish

Coyote lived in a village. The people of the village had no fish to eat. They were hungry.

The people in the next village had fish. They dried it for winter.

One day Coyote said, "I will go to the next village. I will get fish for my people to eat."

When Coyote got to the next village, he said, "My people are hungry. Can they have some of your fish?"

Coyote got a big pile of dried fish from the people of the village.

Coyote started for home. The pile of dried fish was very big. Coyote said to himself, "I have all day to get home. I think I will stop here and sleep in the grass."

Then Coyote went to sleep with the pile of dried fish by his head.

The Yellow Jackets flew down from the mountain. The Yellow Jackets were little, but they took the big pile of fish and flew away with it.

When Coyote got up, he cried, "Who took my fish?"

He went back to the people in the village who had the fish and said, "When I went to sleep, someone took the pile of dried fish."

Coyote got more fish from the people.

Coyote started for home. When he got to the grass where he had had some sleep before, he said to himself, "I will look like I am sleeping, but I will not go to sleep. I will see who took my fish."

The Yellow Jackets came. Coyote did not think the little Yellow Jackets could go off with his fish.

Coyote watched. The Yellow Jackets took the big pile of fish. Then they flew away to the mountain.

Coyote jumped up and ran after them.

The Yellow Jackets got to the top of the mountain. They put the pile of dried fish into a hole in the top of the mountain. Then the Yellow Jackets flew into the hole to eat the fish.

Coyote saw the hole where the Yellow Jackets had put his fish. He started to think. The Yellow Jackets would sting him if he got into the hole.

Coyote said to himself, "I will make a big fire. The smoke from the fire will make the Yellow Jackets come out of the hole. Then they will not sting me, and I can get my fish."

The smoke from the coyote's fire went into the hole at the top of the mountain. But the Yellow Jackets did not come out of the hole.

To this day, Coyote is on top of the mountain. When the people see smoke on top of the mountain, they think, "Coyote started a fire. He wants to smoke the Yellow Jackets out of the hole. He wants to get his fish."

# Coyote and Bear

Bear liked to sleep. So did Coyote, but Coyote could not sleep like Bear. Bear could sleep all winter.

"I would like to sleep all winter, too, like Bear," Coyote said. "I will ask Bear how he can sleep so long. I will ask Bear how I can sleep all winter."

To talk to Bear, Coyote had to walk to Bear's house. Bear's house was a long walk away. It was up on the top of a hill. It was a long walk in the woods to the hill. It was a longer walk up the hill.

"Yes, the walk is long," said Coyote. "But I will go on walking. I will ask Bear how he sleeps all winter."

So Coyote walked.

Coyote had not walked too long when he saw Squirrel up in a tree.

"I would like to sleep all winter," said Coyote to Squirrel. "I will walk to Bear's house to ask him how."

"I would not like to sleep all winter!" said Squirrel. "I like to play in the snow."

"I like to play in the snow too," said Coyote. "But if I play in the snow, I cannot sleep all winter."

Squirrel watched Coyote go up the hill. As he watched, it started to snow.

On the top of the hill, Coyote saw Bear's house. In the window Coyote saw that Bear was going to bed but had not started sleeping.

"Bear," called Coyote. "Help me sleep all winter."

"Roar," said Bear to Coyote.

Coyote was not afraid. "Bear," he called. "Will you help me?"

"Roar!" said Bear.

Coyote was not too afraid. "Bear," he called. "How do I sleep all winter?"

"ROAR!!!!" said Bear.

Coyote was afraid. He started to run down the hill and did not stop! At Squirrel's tree, he called, "I like to play in the snow too. I will not sleep all winter."

Squirrel laughed and watched Coyote run away.

# Coyote and Rattlesnake

Once, Coyote and Rattlesnake were friends. One day Coyote said to Rattlesnake, "Come to my house. We will have something good to eat."

"Thank you," said Rattlesnake. "I will come soon."

The next day Rattlesnake went to Coyote's house. Rattlesnake crawled on the floor. He shook the rattle on his tail.

Coyote watched Rattlesnake. "Here is some good food to eat," said Coyote.

"I do not want food," said Rattlesnake. "I want the yellow flowers of the corn."

So Coyote went out to get the yellow flowers of the corn. He took them to his house.

"Put them on my head," said Rattlesnake. Coyote did not want to go up to Rattlesnake.

Rattlesnake said again, "Come here. Put the yellow flowers of the corn on my head."

Coyote did all that Rattlesnake told him to do.

The next day Rattlesnake came again and said to Coyote, "Come to my house. We will have something good to eat."

"Thank you," said Coyote. "I will come."

Coyote said to himself, "I think Rattlesnake will like me more if I am more like he is."

So Coyote got a rattle and put it on his tail. He crawled on the ground to Rattlesnake's house. He shook and shook the rattle on his tail.

Coyote looked so funny that Rattlesnake wanted to laugh. But Rattlesnake said to himself, "Coyote is very foolish."

He saw that Coyote wanted to be like him. Rattlesnake said to Coyote, "The animals are afraid of my rattle. Do you want me to be afraid of you? Come and eat some food. It is for you."

"I do not want food," said Coyote. "I want the yellow flowers of the corn." Coyote wanted to be just like Rattlesnake.

"This food is very good. It is just for you," said Rattlesnake.

But Coyote said, "Put the yellow flowers of the corn on my head. I will be just like you."

Rattlesnake got some yellow flowers of the corn.

Coyote said, "Come here, and put the yellow flowers of the corn on my head."

"I am afraid," said Rattlesnake. But to himself he said, "Coyote is very foolish. I want to laugh."

Rattlesnake put the yellow flowers of the corn on Coyote's head. Coyote looked very foolish.

Coyote did not eat the good food. He went home hungry.

"I was so foolish," he said to himself. "A coyote cannot be like a rattlesnake. And Rattlesnake had very good food for me. I could have eaten it."

Coyote took the rattle from his tail. Then he went out to look for food. And Coyote did not crawl on the ground again.

# Coyote and Bluebird

Once, Bluebird was not blue. He was the color of dirt. He did not want to be the color of dirt.

Every day Bluebird went into the water to sing.

"Water, Water, make me blue.

Make me as blue as the sky.

Water, Water, make me blue."

Every day Coyote watched Bluebird.

One day when Bluebird got out of the water, he had no feathers. He did not want the other animals to see him. Bluebird was sad and started to sing.

"Water, Water, what did you do?

Water, Water, what did you do?"

Then Water was singing to Bluebird.

"Little Bluebird, I am your friend.

I will make you as blue as the sky.

Little Bluebird, come back to me."

Bluebird got into the water again. When he got out of the water, his feathers were blue.

Coyote saw Bluebird. "Where did you get the pretty blue feathers?" asked Coyote.

"I went into the water," said Bluebird, "and then I was as blue as the sky."

"I want to be a blue coyote," said Coyote. "How can I get the water to make me blue? I am afraid to go into the water."

"You must go into the water, and you must sing to the water," said Bluebird.

Bluebird started to sing.

"Water, Water, make me blue.

Make me as blue as the sky.

Water, Water, make me blue."

Coyote tried to sing. He did what he could, but he was not good at singing.

Every day Coyote jumped into the water. He tried to sing. He was afraid of the water, but every day he went in.

One day Coyote got out of the water. He looked at himself. He was a blue coyote.

Coyote was very proud. He walked in the woods. He was so proud he called to the animals, "Look at me. Look at me. I am a blue coyote."

Coyote walked down the road. He called to the people, "Look at me. Look at me. I am a blue coyote."

Coyote was very proud. He did not look where he was going. He went in the dirt. Coyote had dirt on him from his head to his tail. To this day, Coyote is the color of dirt.